D0758715

THEY DIED TOO YOUNG

SELENA

Veda Boyd Jones

CHELSEA HOUSE PUBLISHERS
Philadelphia

Printed and bound in Malaysia.

3 5 7 9 8 6 4

Photographs courtesy of: AP/Wide World Photos, Archive
Photos, London Features International Ltd. and Photofest.

Cover photo courtesy Photofest

Library of Congress Cataloging-in-Publication Data
Jones, Veda Boyd.
    Selena / Veda Boyd Jones.
        p. cm. – (They died too young)
    Discography: p.
    Includes bibliographical references and index.
    Summary: Discusses the life and work of the award-winning Texas
    singer who had begun to popularize Tejano music when she was
    shot and killed by the president of her fan club.
        ISBN 0-7910-5230-0 (hardcover)
        1. Selena, 1971-1995—Juvenile literature.
    2. Tejano musicians—Biography—Juvenile literature.   [1. Selena,
    1971-1995.   2. Singers.   3. Mexican-Americans—Biography.
    4. Women—Biography.   5. Tejano music]   I. Title.   II. Series.
    ML3930.S43J66   1999
    782.42164—dc21
    [B]   99-11563
                                                                  CIP

Publishing Coordinator Jim McAvoy
Contributing Editors Bruce Durost Fish, Becky Durost Fish
Digital Design, Book Production Robert Gerson

ABOUT THE AUTHOR

Award-winning writer Veda Boyd Jones enjoys the challenge of
writing for a variety of readers. Her published works include nine
adult novels, four children's historical novels, four children's
biographies, a coloring book, and numerous articles and short stories in national magazines. Mrs. Jones, who holds a master's
degree in history from the University of Arkansas, teaches writing
and speaks at writers' conferences. She lives in Missouri with her
husband, Jimmie, and three sons, Landon, Morgan, and Marshall.

CONTENTS

Selena's exciting performances drew thousands of fans

THE QUEEN OF TEJANO

Selena climbed into the open carriage. With a giddyap from the driver, two horses broke into a trot and pulled the carriage into the arena of the Houston Astrodome. Thunderous applause from thousands of fans greeted Selena. Old and young alike had come to see and hear the Tejano singer. She waved from the carriage, her smile big and friendly. The horses stopped by the stage, and Selena bounded up the steps to her band, Los Dinos.

"How ya doin', Houston?" she shouted, and the crowd roared with approval.

Decked out in skintight sparkling purple pants with flared bell-bottoms and a matching bolero-style jacket over a halter top, the black-haired beauty launched into a disco medley including "I Will Survive," "Last Dance," and "On the Radio." Emotion colored her soprano voice. She danced to the music, her silver high heels moving with the beat. She turned, she twirled, and she whirled. She was a part of the music.

The fans who filled the Astrodome on February 26, 1995, were mostly Latinos—Americans who traced their heritage to Mexico or other Central or South American countries. They liked it fine that Selena Quintanilla Perez sang songs in English, but they had come to hear her sing Tejano songs in Spanish.

Tejano is the Spanish word for *Texan* and is the contemporary term for the type of music that has flourished on the Texas-Mexican border since the early 1900s. Tejano is happy music, bouncy, lively, and joyful. Borrowing from the polka sound of German immigrants with their button accordions, it mixes in the Mexican twang of a 12-string guitar. Drums and a bass completed the ensemble in the early days, and the music was called Tex-Mex. Nowadays a keyboard and synthesizer replace the accordions, and electric guitars replace acoustic guitars, but the results are the same—jaunty toe-tapping music.

"Once you start playing Tejano, it's like the Pied Piper, you know? You start dancing," said Flaco Jimenez, a pioneer in the Tex-Mex sound.

At the Astrodome, people danced in the aisles to Selena's Tejano music. Her bubbly personality and genuine desire to entertain her fans had allowed her to break the unspoken rule that women couldn't make it in Tejano music.

Not only was Selena a female singer, she flaunted her femininity in outlandish costumes mimicking rock stars Madonna and Janet Jackson.

"I started wearing cropped shirts, and they started getting higher and higher and then, finally, I was wearing just a bra. Now, it's kind of a gimmick—'Selena wears bras and bolero jackets,'" the star once noted.

Her bra was actually a bustier, decorated with sequins and beads. She loved sewing on the decorations and designing costumes which shouted that she accepted the body she had, even though she'd privately told a friend that she wished her bottom wasn't so big.

Selena used the entire stage, dancing from front to back, side to side. It was her world, and she played brilliantly to the crowd.

"What I do on stage, you won't catch me doing offstage," she said. "I mean, I think deep down I'm still kind of, like, timid and modest about a lot of things. But on stage, I release all that; I let it go."

Her image wasn't just the sexy singer, it was also the girl next door. Her traditional family values were held up as an example by mothers to their daughters.

"We're a very unified family," Selena said. "Within the family we have aggressive and dominating personalities, but we believe the family is the most important thing of all."

The family band was a business, and that was never for-gotten. They all worked together.

"Everybody knows their position in the band, nobody steps over their line as far as my dad's being the manager," Selena once said. "We don't get into business or tell him what to do. My brother creates the music and we let him take care of that. My sister is in charge of the marketing. We don't step over that line. We all have our little jobs. We are just like a team."

Her mother traveled with the group and dispensed advice and love. Selena's job was to captivate the crowd with her voice, her personality, and her showmanship.

She managed her task with no trouble. The Astrodome rocked on Tejano night with 61,000 fans packed in to see Selena and another Tejano singer, Emilio. The huge crowd broke attendance records that Selena had set the previous two years at the Houston Livestock Show and Rodeo and was sec-ond only behind country singer Garth Brooks in all-time atten-dance at a concert in the arena.

The crowd was filled with fans of all ages. Senior citizens moved to the music. Young girls wore flat bustiers. Latino girls wanted to be like Selena, who had set a goal and worked toward it. She was their idol, one of them, and she had made it big.

Selena wasn't content to have made it to the Astrodome. She was working on a crossover album, which would be in English and would widen her marketing base. But she wouldn't forsake her Latino fans. Opening the Astrodome show with an English pop medley was a way of feeling out the Tejano fans. She and her manager-father carefully noted the crowd's reaction to the pop songs.

She had broken into the Latin pop music scene with her records played on Spanish radio stations from California to Florida, and she was one of the few Tejano artists who had accomplished that feat. Now Selena wanted to sing in English.

After all, English was her native language.

*Although exotic onstage, Selena remained
approachable to her fans*

MUSIC IN HER SOUL

In his younger days, Selena's father, Abraham Quintanilla Jr., had been a member of the Dinos (guys), which sang pop tunes in English. The Dinos became Los Dinos when the band realized they could earn more if they sang in Spanish and focused on the Tex-Mex sound. They cut a few records and had some regional hits but never made the big time. Still, the dream of success in the music industry never left Abraham, and he passed that desire to his daughter.

Even after Abraham's marriage to Marcella Samora and the birth of two children, Abraham III (called A.B.) and Suzette, he continued with his music. But family demands required a more reliable income. Abraham quit playing with the band at clubs and took a job with Dow Chemical Company in Lake Jackson, Texas.

A year and a half later on Easter Sunday, April 16, 1971, Marcella gave birth to Selena. Her mother dressed her in frills, and it soon became apparent that this little girl was a bundle of energy.

Harold Lindloff, of the First State Bank in Lake Jackson, recalled Selena as a three-year-old accompanying her parents on trips to the bank. "Everyone had a feeling that she was destined to be more than the average child. She was so beautiful. She was vibrant. The way I remember her, because of her teaching she respected her elders but she always had a twinkle in her eye, you could always cut up with her. She had that aura, something magical."

Her father saw the magic in her, too, and heard in her voice a promise of something special. His love of music led him to teach A.B. how to play the bass guitar. He taught

9

Suzette the drums and put a microphone in Selena's hand. Songs such as "Feelings," "Blue Moon," and "Somewhere Over the Rainbow" became standard songs for the children. Because Selena didn't speak Spanish, her father taught her to sing Spanish lyrics phonetically.

Abraham Quintanilla made his children practice. Many times they would be outside playing in the yard with neighborhood kids when he'd call them inside. They might complain, but they did as they were told and reported to the garage, which was soundproofed with carpet tacked to the walls. Theirs was a close-knit Latino family where the father was the head, and they did what he commanded.

The Quintanillas' neighbor Carmen Read said, "There wasn't a lot of free time for those kids. They may have worked harder and shouldered more responsibilities than their peers, but that did not inhibit Selena's bubbly personality. She would just laugh. Never would she cry, never was she rude or ugly. She just had such a good outlook on life. She was such a happy child."

Selena enjoyed her childhood. "I was a little tomboy when I was growing up. I used to like to play football with the guys and, you know, normal things like hide-and-seek, and get ahold of my brother's bike and try to teach myself to ride it. I hurt myself a couple of times. That's normal."

But her childhood wasn't exactly normal. Selena was fairly popular in school because of her friendliness, but she was sometimes viewed as odd because of her religion. Her grandparents were Jehovah's Witnesses. Selena's parents were not actually members, but they observed the principles of the faith. They did not celebrate birthdays or Christmas. Whenever there was a party at school, Selena went to the library or home.

Selena was also different from her classmates in looks. She was a third-generation American because her father and her father's parents had been born in the United States, but she had Mexican ancestors. Her skin was browner than that of her white classmates, and she had dark eyes and black hair. Those surface differences didn't bother Selena, who viewed herself as an American through and through.

She also had a budding musical career, which set her aside from her classmates. In 1978, Selena and her brother and sister cut a demo 45 record under the name Southern Pearl. Besides performing at any family gathering, they began to play in public. They won $200 in a talent contest at the Wharton County Fair, and Abraham booked them at weddings, birthdays, and other parties. Selena liked the attention, and she found that singing helped her overcome her sense of shyness.

Selena's good friend Meredith Lynn Cappel told reporter Joe Nick Patoski, "We used to love to ask her to sing songs. It gave you chill bumps how powerful her voice was, and this was in third and fourth grade. She'd do it during recess and when we walked home from school. Any Top 40 song she could sing. She didn't just sing it, she really got into it."

Selena did her homework and earned good grades, but that didn't keep a couple teachers from talking to her father about her extracurricular activities. They accused Abraham of child labor, but since the family band only performed on weekends and didn't interfere with her school attendance, he brushed their objections aside.

It wasn't long before the family members were working on weeknights, too, and not just with music. In 1980, Abraham and his friend Santos Serda Jr. opened a Mexican restaurant in Lake Jackson. Selena, A.B., and Suzette bussed tables and generally helped out at Papa Gayo's while their mother and Mrs. Serda ran the kitchen. Abraham quit his job at Dow Chemical to work at the restaurant. Papa Gayo's featured live entertainment Thursdays through Saturdays. The family band played, and the newspaper advertisement for the new restaurant referred to Selena as "the sensational nine-year-old singer."

The band was called Selena and Company when disc jockey Primo Ledesma went to the restaurant. He always carried a tape recorder with him, and with Abraham's permission, he turned it on and taped Selena singing a song in Spanish. Ledesma played it on the air the next day, and the phones rang off the hooks. Listeners wanted to know about this little girl.

The gig for the family band at Papa Gayo's didn't last long. The restaurant lost customers and went out of business in March 1981. The Quintanilla family sold their house and moved in with one of Abraham's brothers in El Campo, where Selena attended school and placed second in the fifth grade spelling bee. The band continued under the name of Los Dinos and expanded its base of Spanish songs that were part of Texas culture. Selena was now singing Tejano music.

The following year the family moved back to Lake Jackson and lived in a small apartment. Abraham entered Selena in Starmania, a local talent search, and she won the qualifying round seven weeks in a row with her version of "Feelings." She continued to do well in school, even though her teachers were concerned about her absences due to musical performances.

Soon Abraham moved the family again, this time to Corpus Christi. He was tired of working temporary jobs that were going nowhere. The way out of poverty had to be music. There were several regional record companies in Corpus Christi, and he was going to need their help if Los Dinos was going to take off. He also had family there, and the population was more than half Latino, a natural audience for the new sound of Los Dinos.

The addition of a keyboard player and another guitarist gave the group more depth. Abraham painstakingly taught Selena more Tejano songs, even though she could barely speak Spanish, only picking up a word here or there.

The common languages in the Corpus Christi area were Spanish, English, and a combination called Spanglish. Selena would use made-up words that used Spanish endings on English words, like *wifa* for *wife*. Sometimes she'd use both languages in the same sentence, such as, *Como se llama* that place? which meant, What's the name of that place? But when it came to singing in Spanish, she did a passable job.

In 1983, Selena cut several 45 records. They got limited airtime on the radio and sold few copies. The real money in Tejano music was from performances. Abraham packed the family into the old van and pulled a homemade trailer that carried the instruments. They traveled across the borderlands of Texas. The band, now billed as Selena y los Dinos, played at dance clubs, parties, and even benefits.

After the group's single record "Oh, Mamá" was recorded and played frequently on the radio, the band made a television appearance on the *Johnny Canales Show*, a variety show broadcast out of Corpus Christi. On the air, Johnny Canales teased Selena about her Spanish, which she still butchered terribly. She laughed and took it in stride.

Selena attended West Oso Junior High School in the working-class neighborhood of Molina, but she frequently missed school on Mondays and Fridays. Those days were required for travel to and from the band's musical gigs. She kept up with her schoolwork and her grades were excellent, but her seventh grade reading teacher, Marilyn Greer, was concerned about Selena's attendance.

"Selena was probably a valedictorian-quality student," Greer later said. "She was not only beautiful, she was very, very intelligent, and she conducted herself like a lady, which coming from the barrio [Latino neighborhood] was not an easy thing to do. You're talking someone who was bright, a minority, and female. This child could have gotten a four-year scholarship with any major university in the country."

Although Ms. Greer spoke with Abraham about his daughter's future, he wouldn't listen. He felt Selena was destined for greatness in music. If necessary, he told the teacher, he would take her out of school.

And that's what he did the following year. He pulled Selena out of eighth grade. Now that her public school education was over, she applied herself to correspondence studies from the American School of Chicago. She was 13.

Life on the road could be lonely, and Selena missed being with kids her own age

ON THE ROAD

Life on the Tejano music circuit became a new kind of normalcy for Selena. Cut off from her old friends at school, Selena's acquaintances were now other musicians and people she met on the road.

Still driving the van and pulling the trailer, Abraham became even more of a stage father than before. From his early days with his own band, he had learned the ins and outs of the music business and knew that some dance club owners skimmed money off the receipts at the door. He argued over dollars and earned a reputation as a hard man to work with, but he was protecting his family. Selena y los Dinos was the family's meal ticket, and many times those meals were quick stops on the road at the nearest burger joint.

Selena would rather have had her favorite pepperoni pizza, but she didn't complain about food. She rarely complained about anything. Her sunny outlook on life kept the family positive and upbeat.

Abraham did not depress the family with financial concerns, even though they all knew that there was little money. What they made went back into sound equipment, costumes, or paid their travel expenses. They cut corners where they could, crowding into motel rooms. When profits came in, they were split four ways between the parents, A.B., Suzette, and Selena.

The band began recording for GP Records and used Manny Guerra's studio. A.B. learned about studio electronics from Manny. Selena's brother excelled at the finer arts of production. For the band's first hit record, "Dame un Beso" ("Give Me a Kiss"), A.B. was composer, arranger, and producer.

At 15, Selena scored her first magazine cover. *Tejano Entertainer* ran two pictures of her on the front: one captured her in an offstage flirtatious pose with her short hair teased up, and in the other one she sang into a microphone and wore mirrored sunglasses. The accompanying story called her the youngest female vocalist on the Tejano circuit.

Other publicity abounded. Ramon Hernandez, a promoter for GP Records, published a fact sheet on Selena, including a list of the band's recordings. He also designed a promo card with pictures of Selena and her family that detailed her favorite things, such as pizza and the television show *Moonlighting.* Her personal philosophy was listed as "Be at your best at all times."

That was not just a publicity quote to Selena. She lived her motto. Her acquaintances were people she met in different towns on the tour. Although months might pass before she saw them again, she always hugged them and remembered their names.

Her role model was her mother. Always in the background, Marcella Quintanilla was an anchor in a world that found Selena on the road as much as she was at home in the Molina neighborhood in Corpus Christi. Selena described her mother as "loving, sentimental, honest, uncomplicated. My mom is everything that is good. I want to be like her."

Besides getting exposure on the tour, the band's music was getting lots of air time on Tejano music radio stations, which played a mix of songs in Spanish and English. "A Million to One" hit the number one spot at a San Antonio station. Listeners in the borderland between Texas and Mexico now knew the young female singer by one name—Selena.

Before she turned 16, Selena won her first big award. The Tejano world was surprised when she took the 1987 Female Vocalist of the Year Award from Laura Canales, the sultry-voiced singer who had won the award for years and was acknowledged as the *reina de la onda* (queen of the wave, an early name for Tejano music). Selena had been nominated two times before, but the win catapulted her toward Tejano stardom.

In April, during the band's second appearance on the *Johnny Canales Show*, Selena looked more sophisticated, with longer hair and more confidence. Again Canales teased her about her inability to carry on an interview in Spanish. Although Selena had picked up quite a few words, she couldn't carry on a full conversation in the language.

Abraham continued to hustle gigs for the band and booked them as the opening act for the two biggest Tejano bands, Mazz from Brownsville and La Mafia from Houston. Both all-male bands had huge sounds systems and flashy light shows. To update their image, Selena y los Dinos created their own light system on their shoestring budget. They placed regular light bulb fixtures in large coffee cans and sprayed them black. Over them they placed colored plastic film that would give the effect they wanted.

In 1988 Selena won her second Female Vocalist of the Year trophy at the Tejano Music Awards. This allowed the band to raise its performance price. Now they made between $300 and $600 a show, and the van and trailer were traded for a bus, nicknamed Big Bertha. It became a home-away-from-home for the band. A.B.'s new wife, Vangie, traveled on the bus with the band and worked the lights alongside Selena's mother.

While her dad drove the bus, Selena did homework for her correspondence courses. When she finished that, she'd work on her costume designs. If she hadn't been a singer, she declared, she would have gone to school to be a fashion designer. She sewed beads and spangles on costumes and drew pictures of different outfits she could wear for special performances. Offstage Selena liked to wear black, but onstage she preferred bright, vivid colors. Her formfitting styles used spandex materials and shiny, sparkly decorations that glittered as she danced with the music.

When A.B. finished a new song, Selena would practice

and practice the lyrics, paying particular attention to the pronunciation of the Spanish words. She'd been criticized for saying the words wrong, and she wanted to get them right. Her father helped her, but she had trouble trilling the *r*s.

Selena told promoter Ramon Hernandez that she missed going to school. "I had a very boring childhood because I never had the opportunity to associate with anybody my own age due to my career. I miss being around kids my own age.

"I've never been to a football game or had a date my entire life." But she'd had marriage proposals. "Sure, fans and admirers write me proposals on notes, but they're in a flirting or joking way.

"As for dancing, I only dance with people I know. I don't dance with strangers unless they ask my dad for permission. I also enjoy seeing other people dance. Then I go backstage and practice the steps I saw."

On a typical day, Selena y los Dinos might perform an afternoon gig in one town and an evening performance in another. After the night performance, Selena and Suzette would be locked on the bus for their safety while the others broke down the set. Then everyone would load up, and the following night they'd be in a different location. They'd spend four or five nights a week on the road. Although they had graduated from small dance halls to large ones, the smoky smell and the dinky dressing rooms seemed the same. On the bright side, everywhere people greeted them with a smile and wanted to dance to their Tejano sound.

In 1989, Selena again won the Female Vocalist of the Year Award at the Tejano Music Awards. After she turned 18 that year, she changed record labels. Capitol-EMI Latin Records had big plans for Selena that included new distribution. She had captivated Tejano fans. Now it was time to widen her appeal. The professionals at EMI saw the road to an English crossover market first winding through the international Latin market. If they could sell her Tejano records in Mexico and in other Central and South American countries, then she could switch to English lyrics and make a big splash in the American rock scene.

For a fuller sound to the band, Abraham hired a male singer to harmonize with Selena and added a second keyboardist. Now Los Dinos's sound was stronger, bolder, and richer. Record sales climbed, and a gig frequently paid as much as $5000.

That same year, after lengthy negotiations, Selena signed on as a spokesperson for Coca-Cola. That deal meant $145,000 a year for the Quintanillas, divided four ways, just as they split all band profit. Besides TV commercials in Mexico, posters of Selena holding a bottle of Coke were to be displayed in stores not just in Texas, but in any area across the United States that catered to Latinos. While 60 percent of Latinos in America traced their roots to Mexico, 12 percent had origins in Puerto Rico, 5 percent in Cuba, and 23 percent in other Central and South American Countries. Coke wanted to reach them all.

The folks at Coke were thrilled with their new spokeswoman. As advertising executive Lionel Sosa said, "This kid had this innate ability to remember everybody's name, be totally gracious, know who everybody was. I've spent all my life trying to figure out politics and who's who and who has the power, and she instinctively knew it. Maybe she didn't know it, but she was just wonderful to everybody, whether it was the assistant at a shoot or the president of Coca-Cola. She knew who everybody was, went out and hugged them, and made it seem like it was a privilege for her to be doing what she was doing. You always got that feeling, like [she thought] I'm so lucky to be here."

Selena exuded confidence and success to young girls

LIFE CHANGES

Selena had grown up. She was no longer the cute little girl who could belt out a Tejano tune. As the decade of the 1990s began, she was a woman with the physical curves to prove it and the mental attitude of someone who wanted to be in charge of herself.

Of course, that was impossible since she was a member of the family band, and her father still held tight rein on it and especially on her. He had objected when her cropped tops crossed the line to bustiers, but he'd come around when he saw her stage presence in the skimpier outfits and the crowd's reaction. He told her she was too trusting of strangers, and he was beside her to protect her from her naiveté. But to her fans, she was a butterfly breaking out of its cocoon.

Selena was not conceited offstage, but onstage she exuded the confidence of a woman who knew where she was going. She realized she had influence with Latino youths, and she used it in positive ways. As a spokesperson for the Texas Prevention Partnership, she talked to school kids about drug and alcohol abuse. Her message was clear: "With a positive attitude, you can be anything you want to be." She told students that if they didn't stay in school, they would be stuck in dead-end jobs if they could find jobs at all.

Young girls wanted to be confident and successful like Selena. Junior high school boys had crushes on the good-looking, sexy young woman who danced across the stage to the music.

As expected, Selena walked away with top female honors at the 1990 Tejano Music Awards. But her music was taking on a different sound, as reflected in her new album at the time, *Ven Conmigo* (Come with Me). Her voice could go from deep and sultry to high soprano, and the album showcased this talent. The cover named Selena as the performer. Los Dinos was written inside in small print as the musicians. Besides the standard Tejano songs, the album included more international Latin music, which was not by accident. It was time for Selena to branch out.

The album hit the top of *Billboard*'s regional Mexican chart and stayed on the chart for 56 weeks. This was the first time a Tejano act, either male or female, had accomplished this feat. The Quintanillas celebrated.

Selena's gender had always been a handicap. Stereotypically, in the Latin culture, the male was the dominant person with the female behind him. Males ran the music industry. Traditionally crowds turned out to see male performers. Now they were turning out to see Selena.

Los Dinos expanded again. This time Abraham hired Chris Perez from San Antonio. He excelled at hard rock, and his mastery of the guitar lent a harder edge to Los Dinos.

A highlight of the year for Selena was receiving her high school degree from the American School of Chicago. All those years of independent study had paid off, but her thirst for knowledge hadn't been quenched. She was accepted for college correspondence courses from a California school. She also was determined to learn Spanish. She had played around with the language, but if she wanted to succeed in the international arena, she needed the second language.

For some time, Selena had performed at events with other Tejano groups, and in the summer of 1991 she shared billing with international talent at the Hispanic State Fair in San Antonio. Association with Latin groups was one more way to build the bridge for her crossover into the international market.

When the band appeared for the third time on Johnny Canales's variety show in 1991, the host commented on her improvement in Spanish. He could also have commented on the changed appearance of the band. They wore black and white fake cowhide outfits that Selena had designed. She wore a bustier, black tights, and calf-high boots, which earned her the nickname of the Hispanic Madonna.

But the similarity between the two singers was in dress only. Selena was very approachable to her fans. She shopped at Wal-Mart and ate lunch at the local Pizza Hut. When fans asked for her autograph, she always signed her name. She was one of them, one of the people, and she didn't forget that, even as her star began to climb. In that way, Selena never changed from the little girl who sang at anniversary and birthday parties.

But in another way, she changed dramatically as she matured. Her black hair was now long and flowing, and her image was that of a sexy singer. Awakening within her was the desire to know guitarist Chris Perez on a deeper level than as a friend. Even though he was a shy young man, he and Selena were able to talk easily. He made her laugh and feel happy just to be near him. But how did he feel about her? She couldn't tell, since he didn't treat her any differently than he had when he'd first joined the band. She turned to A.B. for direction.

Her brother asked Chris what he thought about Selena. Of course, Chris thought she was cool, but that wasn't enough of an answer for A.B. He told the guitarist that Selena was interested in him. Stunned by this, shy Chris turned a bright red. He wasn't dismayed by the fact; he had the same feelings for Selena, but he hadn't known that she cared for him in that special way.

Chris and Selena began seeing each other whenever they could, but they didn't let others know. As long as Selena's dad thought they were together because of band business, he couldn't object to their blooming relationship.

Another special friendship began in 1991. Yolanda Saldivar, 11 years older than Selena, first saw the singer in a concert in San Antonio, Yolanda's hometown. She admired the

Tejano star and wanted to start a fan club. She called Abraham and left nearly a dozen messages on his answering machine, and then she met Suzette, who was in charge of Selena's merchandizing. Open to the thought of having help selling T-shirts and other Selena memorabilia, Suzette introduced the short, heavyset Yolanda to her father.

With Abraham's blessing, Yolanda started Selena's fan club. There were two levels of membership. One was free, and those members were sent a list of where Selena would be performing. The other membership cost $20 and entitled the fan to two T-shirts, posters, and a monthly newsletter that contained interviews with band members and other items of interest to Selena followers. Besides running this enterprise, Yolanda served as Selena's personal assistant, organizing events and parties for Selena in Corpus Christi and San Antonio. She made calls to radio stations before Selena's appearances. Yolanda was a loner, much like Selena, whose absence of friends on the road was a forced necessity. Selena's friends were family and band members, a rather small number. She welcomed newcomer Yolanda, and they formed a close friendship.

Selena's special relationship with Chris took a nose dive when Abraham found them hugging. He immediately fired the guitarist, who moved back to San Antonio to work with another band. Selena was brokenhearted and managed to secretly see Chris whenever she could.

In 1992 Selena won her usual awards at the Tejano Music Awards ceremony. At the event, she sang a duet with Alvaro Torres, a Honduran pop singer and the first non-Tejano singer to perform at the awards. The single of their song "Buenos Amigos" (Good Friends) hit number one on *Billboard*'s Latin chart, giving Selena name recognition in Latin American countries. It was one more step on her quest to crossover into international Latin markets.

On April 2 of that year, Selena told her parents she was going shopping. Instead, she met Chris, and they drove to

*The Riverwalk district of San Antonio, a city where
Selena often performed*

the Nueces County courthouse. A justice of the peace married them after a judge set aside the normal 72-hour waiting period. Selena Quintanilla became Selena Perez.

"Ever since I was a little girl, I'd dreamed of having a big, wonderful wedding, with a long white gown and a bouquet of flowers," Selena later told a friend. "But my love for Chris was so strong. I couldn't wait any longer for us to be husband and wife. I couldn't even wear my nicest dress because that would have made my father suspicious."

Although Abraham was initially upset by the elopement, he eventually accepted it. The newlyweds moved to a brick home in the three-house Quintanilla family compound in the Molina subdivision of Corpus Christi. A.B.'s family lived in the house on one side of Abraham and Marcella, and Selena and Chris lived in the house on the other side.

Selena's wide smile became wider as happiness surrounded her. She had a new husband and a new album out, which was well-received by not only Tejano fans but across the border as well. *Entre a Mi Mundo* (Come into My World) featured various types of songs with something that would appeal to every listener. One song was in English. All the songs were written in-house by band members, most of the songs by A.B., and even one by Selena. A postscript on the album mentioned the fan club and gave Yolanda's address.

The album was doing so well, EMI decided it was time for Selena to venture south into Mexico. In Monterrey, Selena would meet press members who regularly covered the music beat in television, radio, magazines, and newspapers.

Although her Spanish was passable in songs, Selena still was not fluent in the second language. Mexicans were critical of Tejanos who didn't speak their language, so Selena nervously approached the press conference. The people she saw there resembled the folks back home, so she relaxed and greeted each one individually, hugging each of the 35 press members. When they questioned her, she answered as best she could in Spanish with a little English thrown in when she didn't know a Spanish word. Her smile, her friendliness, and her enthusiasm enchanted the press corps, and none of them mentioned her language ability. Their stories about the Tejano artist were flattering, and one newspaper reporter called her "*una artista del pueblo*," an artist of the people.

Later that year, in an interview with San Antonio writer Joseph Harmes, Selena was as charming as she was with the press in Mexico. She told Harmes about her business, Fashions by Selena, that she ran out of her home at 705 Bloomington. She loved to design shiny things such as glittery belts and jewelry. Her plans were for a mail-order catalog, and her dream was to own a boutique.

She wouldn't talk about religion or politics, but mentioned surface things that fans were interested in. Her favorite colors were black and purple. She owned several dogs and even a python. Her husband was teaching her to ride his motorcycle. She'd bungee jumped once on a dare.

She talked about her relationship with her father and mentioned that he had cautioned her to be more wary of people. "I trust too easily. That's my problem. And I end up getting hurt in the long run."

Selena praised the job Yolanda was doing as fan club organizer and president. "Fan clubs can ruin you if you don't have people who take care of it." She stressed that fans would get upset if they sent their money in for membership and didn't get the promised merchandise.

When asked what she'd like people to know about her, Selena answered, "I think I'm a very kindhearted person. Um, I don't like to hurt people's feelings. If I do, it's not intentionally. I'm sincere and very honest. And I feel that nowadays a lot of people have lost that, but I think that starts in the home. My parents have taught me that. Being fair with people."

Selena with her 1994 Grammy Award for Selena Live

FASHION DESIGNS

Selena had charmed the press at her Mexican press conference, but she knew it was time to get serious about learning Spanish if she were to succeed in the international Latin market. She studied hard and visited Mexico City. To learn the language properly, she needed to hear it spoken daily. Her pronunciation and accent improved dramatically.

In February 1993, Selena y los Dinos performed at Memorial Coliseum in Corpus Christi. This was a bigger band than before, with three vehicles required to take crew and equipment to the coliseum. The free concert was recorded for EMI and released in the spring as *Selena Live*. Several numbers, although sung in Spanish, could have been translated as English pop/rock music.

Selena's fame continued to grow. She won more awards at the Tejano Music Awards, including Orchestra Album of the Year, for *Entre a Mi Mundo*. Filming videos was now a part of her annual workload as TV audiences clamored for glimpses of the beautiful woman.

In the fall, the family legally formed Q Productions, registered in Texas as a partnership. At Suzette's September wedding, Selena served her sister as matron of honor, and Yolanda Saldivar, the fan club president, was a bridesmaid. Also that fall, Los Dinos returned to Mexico for a concert, where Selena sang in front of 70,000 fans. It was no fluke that she had become the biggest Tejano act in Mexico; she had worked for it.

A more sophisticated-looking musical group appeared again on Johnny Canales's show. Los Dinos wore Selena's fashions, black pants and black vests over white shirts. For the first time, Johnny Canales couldn't tease Selena about her Spanish. She had by then mastered the language.

Her road to fame had wound through the Latin American world. Now it was time for the English album. The slow process of choosing songs and different producers for each song began. Abraham felt there was no great rush. Tejano had changed drastically in the years since Selena y los Dinos had hit the road. Dance halls had changed to big arena concerts, and Selena had grown with the music.

Selena's second career was also taking off. Whereas the music was a family venture, now she was branching out on her own with her fashion interests. In January 1994, her first store opened in Corpus Christi. Selena, Etc. was a combination boutique and salon of personal care services. A woman could enter in blue jeans and no makeup and exit hours later with a manicure, a facial, a new hairstyle, and a new dress.

The fashions, priced from $30 to $1500, were not strictly Selena's work. She hired Martin Gómez to design creations that were sold under the label, "Designed by Martin Gómez, Exclusively for Selena."

She loved to hang around the store, but her busy music schedule didn't allow that. Instead, she hired her trusted friend Yolanda Saldivar as manager of the boutique while she went on the road. The band performed in New York, Los Angeles, Argentina, the Dominican Republic, Columbia, and Puerto Rico. Wherever Selena went, people loved her.

No stranger to award ceremonies, since she annually won at the Tejano Music Awards, Selena was still surprised to receive a 1994 Grammy nomination for best Mexican-American album for *Selena Live*. She thanked her family, her husband, and her fans when she won the national award.

In April, *Amor Prohibido* (Forbidden Love) was released. Like the others recorded for EMI, this album contained various types of music that would please both traditional and contemporary Tejano fans and Latin music lovers. Most of the songs were written by A.B., but Selena had written "Bidi Bidi Bom Bom," a fluffy melody that soared up the international charts.

More demands were placed on Selena's time, but the self-proclaimed workaholic thrived on new projects. She briefly appeared and sang in the movie *Don Juan DeMarco,* starring Marlon Brando, Faye Dunaway, and Johnny Depp. As spokeswoman for Agree Shampoo and Southwestern Bell's Call Notes, she filmed more commercials. She appeared in a cameo role on two episodes of a Mexican soap opera.

In September, Selena opened her second boutique in San Antonio, which coincided with an issue of *Texas Monthly* that listed Selena as one of the top 20 most important Texans of 1994. That month Q Productions bought a building, and renovations began to turn it into a state-of-the-art recording studio.

Selena admitted she rarely got butterflies before performances, but she was very nervous at the December fashion show in San Antonio that featured her line of clothing. Her tension wasn't visible. A newspaper review of the show called Selena cool and calm and hailed the new line as a hit.

Succeeding in the fashion world was important to Selena. With two stores opened in Texas, she set her sights on expanding. If she could find a manufacturer in Mexico, she could lower her costs and prices and widen her customer base. Perhaps she could later open a store there.

She and Yolanda made several trips to Monterrey, investigating the possibilities. But things at the boutiques were not going well. Cancellation of personnel's insurance led to questions, but Yolanda said she'd take care of it. Selena's designer, Gómez, accused Yolanda of not paying bills and of destroying some of his designs. Yolanda was becoming possessive of Selena and denying others access to her.

Gómez and Abraham advised Selena to get rid of Yolanda, but Selena dismissed their opinions. How could this wonderful friend, who was always there to see to Selena's needs, not be a good person?

Yolanda had even given her a ring that had been designed especially for Selena. Because she'd been born on Easter Sunday, Selena had a fondness for eggs and collected handcrafted egg designs. The special friendship ring featured a white gold-encrusted egg surrounded by 52 tiny diamonds. Selena wore it on her right index finger. She said everyone could see it there, since she held the microphone in that hand.

However, Selena didn't wear the ring at the Houston Astrodome in February 1995, when she took the stage for her biggest concert in Texas.

She was nominated for a second Grammy Award for *Amor Prohibido,* and although she didn't win, she was getting national recognition.

Sold-out performances, number one albums, numerous awards, and a career in fashions meant that Selena's wildest dreams were coming true.

At a party with fellow pop singer Jon Secada

Performing at the Alamodome in San Antonio, a week before her death in 1995

BLACK FRIDAY

By March, evidence of embezzlement by Yolanda Saldivar had piled up. Besides accusations by former staff members at Selena, Etc., Abraham had received letters and calls from fans who had joined the fan club and not received the promised merchandise. He called Selena, Suzette, and Yolanda to a March 9 meeting. He asked many questions, but Yolanda had no explanations. Suzette accused Yolanda of being a liar and a thief, but Selena couldn't believe that her trusted friend had turned on her.

The next day Abraham banned Yolanda from Q Productions, but she still worked for Selena's fashion business. Besides contacting financial backers for the expansion of the clothing line in Monterrey, Yolanda was also involved in the choice of a perfume that would bear Selena's name. When those projects were completed, Selena planned to sort out what was happening with Yolanda. As a first step, Selena removed Yolanda's name from the checking accounts for the design business and the boutiques.

On March 26, Yolanda returned to Monterrey and tried to withdraw money from several Mexican checking accounts. A bank teller phoned Selena, and then Selena spoke with Yolanda. She asked that Yolanda return bank statements, a cellular phone, and some perfume samples.

Selena was confused. She had trusted this woman as her best friend and as a business associate. She had taken her into her family, given her gifts, and confided in her. Why was Yolanda betraying her?

When Yolanda returned to Corpus Christi on Thursday

evening, March 30, she checked into the Days Inn and called Selena's beeper. Selena didn't immediately respond. Instead, she fixed supper for Chris and his father, who was visiting them. Around eleven o'clock, she called Yolanda and said she was coming over to get the bank statements. Tax time was nearing, and she needed the financial records. Once she had them, Selena intended to fire Yolanda.

Chris drove Selena to the motel and waited in his truck while she walked into the motel room. The two women had a polite, formal conversation, and Yolanda handed over the needed documents. Once back in the truck, Selena flipped through the pile and discovered that some bank records were still missing.

At home, Selena looked carefully through the papers and became more and more upset. She needed to settle this dispute with Yolanda, but she had to have all of the documents. When Yolanda paged her, Selena called her back.

Yolanda told Selena that she needed to go to the hospital. She claimed she'd been abducted in Monterrey on Wednesday, raped, and some of the records had been stolen. That's why some of the statements were missing.

It was nearly midnight. If this attack had occurred the day before, Chris told Selena, then Yolanda had had plenty of time to seek medical aid. It could wait until the following morning.

On Friday morning, March 31, Selena, dressed in workout sweats, tiptoed out of the house before eight o'clock. She had a lot to do that day, and she wanted the ordeal with Yolanda off her mind. She called Yolanda from the pickup truck and told her she was coming to the motel.

This was a woman who had been so kind to Selena. She'd started the fan club and had turned her house in San Antonio into a virtual shrine with huge pictures of Selena, blowups of her album covers, and other memorabilia. What had happened to turn this dear friend into someone who couldn't be trusted?

After Selena arrived at the motel, she escorted an upset and nervous Yolanda to the hospital. Yolanda was examined; two nurses told Selena out of Yolanda's hearing that the results were inconclusive. They could not confirm that she had been raped. Had Yolanda made up this story to gain sympathy?

On the way back to Yolanda's room, Selena answered her cellular phone. It was Chris, reminding her that she was to be at the studio to record another song for the English crossover album. Abraham, A.B., and Suzette were waiting for her. Selena said she'd be there as soon as she could.

The two women went inside room 158. Harsh words were exchanged, and Selena held out the egg-shaped ring that Yolanda had given her. She would not keep this token of friendship when things had fallen apart between them.

Yolanda pulled a gun from her purse. She aimed it at her own head, and then she pointed the gun at Selena, who turned to run. Yolanda pulled the trigger, and the .38-caliber bullet struck Selena in her right shoulder.

Even though she'd been shot, Selena managed to run out the door, past the swimming pool, and down a long walkway to the motel office.

"Help me! Help me! Call the police!" she screamed to Shawna Vela and Ruben DeLeon, two employees of the motel, as she stumbled into the lobby.

"Help you what?" Vela asked, confused.

"I've been shot!" Selena was now bleeding profusely, and she collapsed on the floor.

The two motel workers didn't recognize her and asked who had shot her.

"Yolanda—158," Selena gasped, and then she passed out.

The motel manager called 911, and an ambulance responded within three minutes.

Paramedic Richard Fredrickson said an egg-shaped ring fell out of Selena's clenched fist in the ambulance when he moved her arm to start an IV. Although he saw a straight line on Selena's heart monitor, indicating no electrical impulses, she was given four units of blood at the hospital in an attempt to revive her.

The Quintanilla family rushed to the hospital. Abraham

Selena's fans mourn her death in Hollywood

objected when he learned Selena had been given blood, since Jehovah's Witnesses didn't believe in that practice, but it was too late anyway. The doctor recorded the time of death as 1:05 P.M. The cause of death was internal bleeding and cardiac arrest, due to a gunshot wound to the back.

At the Days Inn, Yolanda had followed Selena outside, still pointing the gun at her. Then she darted back inside the room and came out again with the gun wrapped in a cloth. Jumping into her pickup, she raced around the parking lot looking for Selena. She pulled into a parking space and locked the doors. When police approached her, she first denied involvement in the shooting, then held the gun to her head, threatening suicide.

Rumors of Selena's death spread fast. Radio stations confirmed the news. At West Oso High School in Selena's Molina neighborhood, the principal announced her death on the intercom system after news of the shooting had flown fast and furious in the halls. He put an end to the speculation, then closed his office door and cried.

Cars were backed up for more than a mile from Selena's home on Bloomington Street. The chain link fence around A.B.'s, Abraham's, and Selena's homes became a memorial as mourners left balloons, ribbons, posters, notes, and drawings. Flowers and candles were left at Selena's two boutiques.

A radio station in San Antonio announced a candlelight vigil for Selena at seven o'clock that night. Five thousand people, young and old, held lighted candles in the dark and listened as disc jockey Jon Ramírez remembered Selena as

They Died Too Young

a superstar who never behaved like one. An air of respect and mourning hung over the crowd. Across town another vigil was held by a competing radio station.

Back in Corpus Christi, Yolanda still held the gun to her head. She sobbed to police over a cellular phone and said that she hadn't meant to kill Selena. She claimed that Abraham hated her and made her shoot Selena, because he was coming between them. Around 9:30 that evening, after nine and a half hours, she climbed out of the cab and gave herself up.

The family and the entire Tejano community were in shock. Surely their beloved Selena wasn't gone. On Sunday, nearly 60,000 people filed

AP Photo

Young mourners pray outside Selena's home in Corpus Christi, Texas

past her closed coffin at the Bayfront Convention Center. Although the doors hadn't opened until nine o'clock, the line started forming at four o'clock that morning. By evening a rumor spread through the crowd that Selena wasn't dead and that the coffin was empty. To dispel the rumor, the family had the casket opened for the last hour of viewing. There lay Selena, her stilled hands holding a white rose, her favorite flower.

In Los Angeles, 4,000 people attended a special Mass for Selena. Another thousand gathered at a Mass in Lake Jackson, Selena's hometown. It didn't matter that Selena wasn't Catholic. She was still one of the people.

On Monday, 600 invited guests attended the graveside services, which were televised by San Antonio and Corpus Christi stations. Mourners placed 8,000 flowers on her coffin before it was cleared and lowered into the ground.

Candles flicker around a memorial to Selena at DeLeon Plaza in Victoria, Texas

SELENA'S LEGACY

The queen of Tejano was gone, but her music would live on. Stores sold out of her CDs, and EMI was pressing millions of copies to meet the high demand. Ironically, many of the stores that now carried her records had not carried them before her death.

Mourning continued. Texas Governor George W. Bush declared April 16, 1995, as *el día de Selena*, Selena Day. She would have been 24 on that day, and it was also Easter Sunday, just as on the day when she was born in 1971. A thousand fans gathered at her grave to sing "Las Mañanitas," the traditional Mexican birthday song. A few miles away at a concert park, 3,000 people attended a Votive Mass of Resurrection for Selena. Many of her fans were Catholic, and this was their way of finding peace with her death.

National magazines featured articles about Selena and her music. *People* magazine carried a Selena cover in Texas. It immediately sold out, so the magazine announced a special tribute issue to be published April 24. The commemorative issue, which sold nearly a million copies, was the third of its type the magazine had ever printed. The other two had honored Audrey Hepburn and Jacqueline Kennedy Onassis.

The Quintanilla family coped the best they could. Abraham ran the licensing of Selena memorabilia; Suzette took over the management of Selena, Etc. Marcella held the family together with love and faith. Chris, always a loner, struggled to get a handle on his grief. A.B. set to work on the English crossover album, *Dreaming of You*. It had been Selena's dream, and it would be her legacy. Her gift was her music, and it would be brought to the world.

AP Photo

*Some of the thousands of young girls waiting in line at the **Selena** movie auditions in Los Angeles. Additional auditions were also held in San Antonio, Miami, and Chicago*

Selena had recorded only four new songs for the English album: "I Could Fall in Love," "Dreaming of You," "Captive Heart," and "I'm Getting Used to You." To complete the album, nine previously released songs were chosen: "God's Child," "Missing My Baby," "Amor Prohibido," "Wherever You Are," "Techno Cumbia," "El Toro Relajo," "Como La Flor," "Tu Solo Tu," and "Bidi Bidi Bom Bom."

Media hype hit a frenzied level over the July 18 release. Some music stores opened a minute after midnight for fans who waited impatiently for the album. More than 210,000 copies were sold the first day; 331,155 were sold in the first week. *Dreaming of You* debuted at number one on the *Billboard* top album chart. It was the first time a Latin artist had achieved that honor.

Reviews of *Dreaming of You* were very much alike. Peter Watrous of the *New York Times* summed it up when he wrote that her English songs were "all competent, but undistinguished. And, oddly enough, the Spanish-language hits, even the light-weight 'Bidi Bidi Bom Bom,' sound better than the English-language tracks. It's the expression of a border culture in the modern age, where musicians can pick and

They Died Too Young

MARCELLA QUINTANILLA

ABRAHAM QUINTANILLA JR.

Selena's parents, Abraham and Marcella Quinatanilla, introduce the actresses who will play their daughter in the film **Selena**. *Portraying the young Selena was 10-year-old Becky Lee Meza of Texas, and actress Jennifer Lopez starred as the adult Selena*

choose what they want to be, how they want to sing. There's a power in the music that isn't so evident in the English-language songs, pieces that could have been sung by any-body, at any place and at any time."

The album was an anthology of Selena. Because she didn't have time to complete the English cuts and her Spanish-language hits were included, she had introduced Tejano music to mainstream America.

Selenamania ruled, but still there was no closure for her many fans. Why was their idol taken from them? They needed answers, and they turned to Yolanda Saldivar's trial. Yolanda's lawyer had convinced a judge that she could not receive a fair trial in Corpus Christi, so it was moved to Houston.

On October 9, jury selection began. Six women and six men were chosen as jurors. Yolanda's lawyer argued that the gun had gone off accidentally. The prosecuting attorney said it was premeditated murder. Yolanda bought the gun after the fateful March meeting with Abraham, Suzette, and Selena, when she could tell that her relationship with the Quintanilla family was unraveling.

After two weeks, the trial was over. In less than three hours, the jury found Yolanda guilty of first degree murder. Outside the courthouse, hundreds of fans celebrated. Music blared, horns honked, and fans cheered. Many danced in the street.

Sadness was mixed with the revelry. Fan Trino Zital said, "All of us in the Spanish-speaking countries will never have a full heart." Another merrymaker said Yolanda Saldivar "thinks she killed Selena, but she only made her more alive, because more people know of her now."

The celebration scene outside the courthouse was repeated a few days later when Yolanda Saldivar was sentenced to life in prison for killing Selena.

Could her fans find closure now? Abraham didn't think so and planned a movie about his daughter's life. He served as executive producer and controlled many aspects of the film. He wanted to keep Yolanda out of the movie, but director Gregory Nava had the final say. "One reason for doing the film was that the fans need catharsis, and if you don't show her death, you can't get that."

Open auditions were held for the part of Selena, both as a young girl and as an adult. Twenty-two-thousand would-be actresses turned out, but in the end the adult part was given to actress Jennifer Lopez. "It's the most difficult role I've had, because Selena isn't a fictional character—and her family is sitting right in front of me while I'm acting. I have never been on a movie set quite like this. It's common to be walking around and find people crying," Lopez said during production.

The script called for several crowd scenes. How difficult would it be to get thousands of fans to reenact the Houston concert? Director Oliver Stone said that the most people he ever got to turn up when he filmed *The Doors* was 3,000, and he had paid them as extras. Associate producers Nancy De Los Santos and Carolina Caldera were in charge of finding 30,000 Selena fans for a concert scene, and they were paying them nothing.

They put ads on radio and television stations, stuffed flyers in mailboxes, tacked posters to telephone poles, and left

Actress Jennifer Lopez as the Tejano singer Selena Quintanilla in a scene from the movie **Selena**

information at schools, restaurants, and beauty shops. De Los Santos said, "The most surprising discovery was that almost all of the hundreds of people we spoke to had seen Selena perform in person, and most either had a snapshot of her or a story to share. We were told she had let their kids dance onstage or she had stayed long after the other bands had left, just to sign autographs. Selena's fans reflected the love that she had for them."

Nearly 33,000 fans turned up for the Astrodome scene. "We came for Selena, even though we know no one can replace her," said fan Yvonne Romero, who arrived at 3:00 A.M. to make sure she got a spot at the "concert."

Before the movie premiere on March 14, 1997, a wave of Selena merchandise hit stores. Along with posters, coffee mugs, and calendars were foot-tall dolls of Selena that sold out in hours.

The film, also starring Edward James Olmos as Abraham and Jon Seda as Chris, opened to mixed reviews, but took in $21.7 million in the first 10 days of release. It has since become available on video and plays regularly on premium cable television channels.

In the movie, Abraham tells Selena, "Listen, being Mexican-American is tough. . . . We've got to be twice as perfect as anybody else.

"We gotta prove to the Mexicans how Mexican we are, and we gotta prove to the Americans how American we are. We've got to be more Mexican than the Mexicans and more American than Americans, both at the same time."

As a Mexican-American, Selena Quintanilla Perez could not make it on the American pop scene without first capturing the Spanish-speaking market. She crossed the line from Tejano music to international Latin music and to English-language music. That she succeeded in doing both reflects on her singing ability and her genuineness.

Since Selena's death, her fashion ventures have taken off. In the summer of 1998, selected Sears and J.C. Penney stores unveiled a new line of Selena fashions aimed at teenagers and their budgets—most items were under $25.

Selena, a woman of the border, left her mark on her entire country. She introduced millions of people to Tejano music, and she touched many lives with her beautiful voice and her beautiful heart.

Chronology

1971 Born in Lake Jackson, Texas, on April 16, Easter Sunday.
1978 Records her first demo 45 record; the band is called Southern Pearl.
1980 Performs as Selena and Company at her father's Papa Gayo's Mexican restaurant.
1983 Moves to Corpus Christi, Texas; by now the band is called Los Dinos.
1987 Wins her first Female Vocalist of the Year Award at Tejano Music Awards at the age of 15.
1989 Becomes a spokeswoman for Coca-Cola.
1990 Receives high school diploma by correspondence from American School of Chicago.
1992 Marries guitarist Chris Perez on April 2; takes press tour of Mexico.
1994 Wins Grammy Award for *Selena Live*.
1995 Appears in film *Don Juan DeMarco*; shot and killed by Yolanda Saldivar on March 31 in Corpus Christi; English crossover album, *Dreaming of You*, debuts at number one on *Billboard*'s album chart.
1997 Film *Selena* premieres.

Major Albums

1989 *Selena y los Dinos* (Capitol-EMI)
1992 *Entre a Mi Mundo* (Capitol-EMI)
1993 *Selena Live* (EMI Latin)
      Mis Mejores Canciones/17 Super Exitos (EMI Latin)
1994 *Amor Prohibido* (EMI Latin)
      12 Super Exitos (EMI Latin)
      Selena (Cema)
1995 *Dreaming of You* (EMI Latin)
1997 *Selena* (Soundtrack) (EMI Latin)

INDEX